YO-YO
MA

INTERNATIONALLY ACCLAIMED CELLIST

YO-YO
MA
INTERNATIONALLY ACCLAIMED CELLIST

by Myra Weatherly

Content Adviser: Joshua Koestenbaum,
Associate Principal Cello,
Saint Paul Chamber Orchestra

Reading Adviser: Rosemary Palmer, Ph.D.,
Department of Literacy, College of Education,
Boise State University

Compass Point Books ✦ Minneapolis, Minnesota

Compass Point Books
3109 West 50th Street, #115
Minneapolis, MN 55410

Visit Compass Point Books on the Internet at *www.compasspointbooks.com*
or e-mail your request to *custserv@compasspointbooks.com*

Editor: Jennifer VanVoorst
Page Production: Blue Tricycle
Photo Researcher: Svetlana Zhurkin
Cartographer: XNR Productions, Inc.
Library Consultant: Kathleen Baxter

Art Director: Jaime Martens
Creative Director: Keith Griffin
Editorial Director: Carol Jones
Managing Editor: Catherine Neitge

Library of Congress Cataloging-in-Publication Data
Weatherly, Myra.
   Yo-Yo Ma : internationally acclaimed cellist / by Myra Weatherly.
      p. cm. — (Signature lives)
   Includes bibliographical references and index.
   ISBN-13: 978-0-7565-1879-0 (library binding)
   ISBN-10: 0-7565-1879-2 (library binding)
   ISBN-13: 978-0-7565-1983-4 (paperback)
   ISBN-10: 0-7565-1983-7 (paperback)
   1. Ma, Yo-Yo, 1955– —Juvenile literature. 2. Violoncellists—
Biography—Juvenile literature. I. Title. II. Series.
   ML3930.M11W43 2006
   787.4'092—dc22
   [B]   2006027356

MODERN AMERICA

Starting in the late 19th century, advancements in all areas of human activity transformed an old world into a new and modern place. Inventions prompted rapid shifts in lifestyle, and scientific discoveries began to alter the way humanity viewed itself. Beginning with World War I, warfare took place on a global scale, and ideas such as nationalism and communism showed that countries were taking a larger view of their place in the world. The combination of all these changes continues to produce what we know as the modern world.

Yo-Yo Ma

Table of Contents

The Strings Sing Out 9

A Musical Prodigy Is Born 17

Starting a New Life 27

Growing Pains 37

Expanding Horizons 47

On the Road 55

Stretching Musical
Boundaries 65

Making Connections 77

Traveling the Silk Road 85

Life and Times 96
Life at a Glance 102
Additional Resources 103
Glossary 105
Source Notes 106
Select Bibliography 108
Index 109
Image Credits 112

1 THE STRINGS SING OUT

⸜⸌⸜⸌⸜

With bow in one hand and cello in the other, Yo-Yo Ma stood on a stage in Washington, D.C. A burst of thunderous applause filled the air. Like a true pro, he acknowledged the continuing applause with repeated bows. His cello performance had left the audience stunned. After all, Yo-Yo was only 7 years old. His 11-year-old sister, Yeou-Cheng, accompanied him on piano.

Just before the concert on November 29, 1962, the usually self-assured Yo-Yo seemed a bit nervous. Backstage at the National Guard Armory, the boy's father began questioning the young cellist. His mother later wrote about the incident:

Are you scared?" his father asked.

The internationally acclaimed cellist Yo-Yo Ma has been performing publicly since he was just 5 years old.

"A little"

"What are you scared of? You know your music perfectly well."

"It's not that. It's that ..."

"The large size of the audience, perhaps?" Five thousand people were expected to attend.

The cello is a stringed instrument and a member of the violin family. It has been in existence for more than 450 years. The cello is much larger than a violin and smaller than a bass. Like the violin, it has four strings. It produces sound when the strings are plucked or when a bow is drawn across them. The cello's range extends to a much lower pitch than the violin. It is played in an upright position between the legs of the seated musician and resting on a metal spike. The fine cellos handcrafted in Italy during the 18th century are worth millions of dollars today.

"Oh, no. Not that. It is just that my cello is small and I'm scared that the sound will not be loud enough for all those people to hear."

His father chuckled and reassured him. "Don't worry about that, there will be loud speakers."

Yo-Yo went on to give a dazzling performance. The enthusiastic audience revealed there had been no cause to worry. Distinguished dignitaries included the president of the United States, John F. Kennedy, and the first lady, Jacqueline. That night, the large audience in Washington's National Guard Armory heard Yo-Yo's cello sing out. And so did thousands of listeners across the nation who watched over closed-circuit television.

Closed-circuit television was the

President and Mrs. Kennedy were guests of honor at An American Pageant of the Arts.

forerunner to pay-per-view television. The program, called *An American Pageant of the Arts*, was broadcast in 75 cites throughout the United States and Canada. Yo-Yo and his cello playing made a big hit with the television audiences. That night, much of the United States discovered the talented musician in one of television's first specials.

The famous American composer Leonard Bernstein conducted the National Symphony Orchestra. Other performers included tenor Richard Tucker and actor Danny Kaye. Yo-Yo and his sister

Leonard Bernstein (1918–1990) was one of America's most popular and accomplished conductors.

were the youngest performers on the program. The show was a huge success.

The following day, rave reviews of Yo-Yo's performance appeared in newspapers. *The Washington Post* ran a picture of him with his cello, which stood almost as tall as the young musician. Reviewers praised Yo-Yo for his extraordinary talent. The media also noted his amazing memory and marveled at his natural feel for being on stage. An article in *The New York Times* described Yo-Yo and his sister as "young virtuosi of the cello and piano."

The concert kicked off a fund-raising campaign for the building of a national cultural center in Washington, D.C. The nation's capital had long been known as a cultural desert, and the new center was designed to change that. In the late 1950s, Congress had decided to build a performing arts center, but lack of funds stalled the plans. When Kennedy became president of the United States, the plans gained momentum because he and his wife strongly supported the campaign. *An American Pageant of the Arts* was part of the plan to fund the building of the center with money from private sources.

On November 22, 1963, nearly one year to the day of the fund-raiser, President Kennedy was assassinated. Since the late 1960s, the performing arts center he did so much to build has stood in Washington, D.C. This cultural center, overlooking the Potomac River, now bears his name. The John F. Kennedy Center for the Performing Arts is a living memorial

The dream of having a national cultural center in Washington, D.C., became a reality on September 8, 1971. This date marked the official opening of the John F. Kennedy Center for the Performing Arts, a memorial to President Kennedy. The former president once said: "The life of the arts, far from being an interruption, a distraction, in the life of a nation, is very close to the center of the nation's purpose." Yo-Yo Ma has peformed numerous times on the stage at the Kennedy Center.

The John F. Kennedy Center for the Performing Arts brought culture to the nation's capital.

to the former president. It is also the nation's performing arts center.

The benefit concert held that November day raised more than $1 million for the building of the arts center. It also brought much publicity and fame to young Yo-Yo Ma. All the attention showered upon such a young child might have proved disastrous, but not for Yo-Yo. He took it all in stride and resolved to "work even harder to master his instrument, to make those strings 'sing out' the music he felt in his soul."

Yo-Yo Ma has gone on to become one of the most widely celebrated musicians in the world. His superstar status puts him on the same level as that of a rock star or a famous athlete. Why is he so famous? One reason is that he has performed with most of the major symphony orchestras in the world. He balances these performances with recital and chamber music activities. He is also an award-winning recording artist. In addition, Ma uses the cello to popularize other musical styles. He plays jazz, tango, and Appalachian fiddle music, and he loves African music. Because of his appearances on children's television, his fans include children as well as adults.

At age 7, Yo-Yo Ma performed in a concert to promote and preserve American culture. As an adult, he focuses on exploring musical cultures worldwide. The gifted cellist says:

> *In the course of twenty-five years of performing in different parts of the world, I have become increasingly intrigued by the migration of ideas among communities. In my musical journey, I have learned from a wealth of different voices.* ❧

2 A MUSICAL PRODIGY IS BORN

❧✦❧

Yo-Yo Ma was born in Paris, France, on October 7, 1955. In Chinese, *Yo* means "friend." The surname *Ma* means "horse." *Yo Ma* translates into "friendly horse." Ma later joked that his parents got lazy and, unable to think of anything else, simply added another "Yo." However, his mother claims that *Yo* did not sound musical enough, so they doubled it. The melodious name—Yo-Yo—rolled easily off the tongue.

Yo-Yo's parents had fled to Paris from China. Both left their homeland to escape the dangerous conditions in war-torn China. Yo-Yo's father, Hiao-Tsiun Ma, was born in a small city near Shanghai in 1911. Yo-Yo's mother, Ya-Wen Lo, was born in 1923 in Hong Kong, an island off the coast of China. Ya-Wen

The Eiffel Tower is recognized around the world as a landmark of Paris, France.

and Hiao-Tsiun grew up in middle-class families.

From an early age, Hiao-Tsiun loved music. He learned to play the violin. He was very talented, and his parents pushed him to devote his life to music. Eventually, he became a music professor at Nanjing University. In 1936, Hiao-Tsiun, along with many other highly educated Chinese, left China to escape the political and cultural unrest. Hiao-Tsiun went to Paris to further his musical studies.

Like his father, Yo-Yo's mother, Ya-Wen Lo, was also devoted to music. As a young child, she studied music and voice, and her dream was to become an opera singer. During World War II (1939–1945), Ya-Wen tried to concentrate on her vocal studies, but it was difficult. Food was scarce, and violence flourished. Her father feared for her safety and insisted that she leave Hong Kong. Ya-Wen went to the mainland to study opera at Central University in Chungking.

As fate would have it, Ya-Wen's professor of music theory was none other than Hiao-Tsiun Ma. Recently returned from Paris, he now taught music at the university. Ya-Wen soon developed a schoolgirl crush on her handsome professor, but Hiao-Tsiun had no clue.

World War II ended in 1945, but peace did not return to China. Disillusioned, Hiao-Tsiun went back to Paris and continued his studies at the University of

Yo-Yo Ma's mother, Ya-Wen Lo, attended university in Chungking, China.

Paris. In time, he earned a doctorate in musicology, the study of music. With his doctoral degree came a new name—Dr. Hiao-Tsiun Ma.

Meanwhile, Ya-Wen grew tired of the violence in China. She decided to go to Paris to study voice. First, however, she returned to Hong Kong to spend time with her family and earn money to pay for her moving expenses.

In 1949, Ya-Wen, at the age of 26, arrived in Paris. She promptly looked up her former teacher. The two became reacquainted and soon developed a close relationship. Hiao-Tsiun Ma and Ya-Wen Lo married on July 17, 1949, and remained in Paris. Ya-Wen began using the French name Marina.

The newlyweds enjoyed the artistic and cultural atmosphere of Paris. The city had received little structural damage from World War II, and many famous landmarks remained intact.

Unfortunately, the war shattered the economy of Paris. The Mas found it hard to make ends meet. Hiao-Tsiun Ma received a meager salary from the university, so to earn extra money, he taught private music lessons. The family also got financial help from Ma's brother, Hiao-Jone Ma, who sent money regularly from the United States. Even so, making a living was difficult.

Baby Yo-Yo, his 4-year-old sister Yeou-Cheng, and his parents lived in a one-room unheated apartment. When temperatures dropped below freezing, the icy room was no place for a baby, so the family moved to a heated hotel room. Hiao-Tsiun took on more students to pay the rent. What they did not know was that the heat was shut off at night in the new room to save costs. Huddled in their frigid room, they survived the winter. Soon after, they moved to larger quarters—two rooms.

From the cradle, Yo-Yo heard music all around him. He listened to recordings of classical music from composers such as Bach and Mozart. Music performed by his father and sister rang out in the small apartment. Young Yeou-Cheng played both violin and piano. Very quickly Yo-Yo showed a talent for music.

As a toddler, Yo-Yo loved to sing. His favorite song was about a jumping frog. While he sang—always in

Composer Wolfgang Amadeus Mozart (1756– 1791) was a child prodigy.

tune—he leaped about like a frog. His opera-trained mother questioned her 2-year-old child as to how he knew when the pitch was too high or too low. Yo-Yo replied that he didn't know how he knew—somehow he just did.

Fun-loving Yo-Yo was also mischievous. While Yeou-Cheng practiced piano, he crawled around her feet. He delighted in holding down the pedals so that she could not use them. One day, his father warned Yo-Yo not to go into the studio while his sister practiced. Outwitting his father, he stood in the doorway and pelted his sister with spitballs.

Despite Yo-Yo's antics, Yeou-Cheng valued his opinion. After her first violin concert at the University of Paris, she asked her 3-year-old brother if he liked her performance. Yo-Yo thought for a moment and said, "[Y]ou played very well. … But you were just a little off tone."

Hiao-Tsiun and Marina knew that Yo-Yo was highly gifted. They also realized that he was a budding prodigy. But did they want their son to have a career in music? They thought about their own poverty and struggles in the competitive field of music. After much soul-searching, they made a decision: They would provide Yo-Yo with a good education in music but would not push him to turn professional.

Yo-Yo's first teacher was Hiao-Tsiun, who started his son on the piano and the violin. Yo-Yo showed talent in both, but his father sensed that Yo-Yo didn't care much for either instrument. Little Yo-Yo admitted, "I don't like the sound violins make; I want a big instrument."

Months passed, and his desire for a "big instrument" persisted. When his father brought home a cello, Yo-Yo jumped for joy. Even a small

The cello is a large stringed instrument played by a seated musician.

cello appeared big to a tiny boy. Lessons began immediately.

To teach Yo-Yo, Hiao-Tsiun used the methods he had developed for teaching music to his young students. His method broke everything down into small pieces. At the outset, he introduced his son to composer Johann Sebastian Bach, one of the most important composers in the history of music. Bach's compositions challenge the ear, the fingers, and the mind of any musician. The young cellist quickly took to Bach. At the age of 4, Yo-Yo mastered selections from Bach's *Six Suites for Unaccompanied Cello*. He not only played the suites—he also memorized them.

Yo-Yo's father made the difficult task easier by having Yo-Yo learn and memorize just two measures each day. Each measure contained just a few notes. Practice sessions were short—no more than 10 minutes. By the end of two days, Yo-Yo knew four measures. By the third day, he knew six and so on until he learned the entire composition.

Yo-Yo's studies progressed

Johann Sebastian Bach was a German musician and composer. Born into a musical family, he received his earliest musical instruction from his father, as did Yo-Yo Ma. During his lifetime, he enjoyed more fame as an organist than as a composer. Bach created choral and instrumental music. More than 1,000 of his compositions survive, including his highly acclaimed Six Suites for Unaccompanied Cello. *Yo-Yo Ma learned to play Bach's cello suites as a very young child and has continued to play the pieces throughout his career.*

Johann Sebastian Bach (1685–1750) is considered to be one of the greatest composers in Western music.

rapidly. At the age of 5, he gave his first public performance. He played both piano and cello at a concert at the University of Paris. Although scheduled to play one movement from the Bach cello suites, he ended up playing all six. He just wouldn't stop playing. Quick-thinking Yo-Yo played the five unscheduled movements as a series of encores.

The Paris performance marked the beginning of major life changes for young Yo-Yo Ma. Soon he would be playing in another country. ✌

3 STARTING A NEW LIFE

Chapter

꒰꒱

Earlier Hiao-Tsiun had been opposed to a professional musical career for young Yo-Yo. But now, thrilled by his son's recital performance, he decided that the time had come to promote such a career. Marina had also initially resisted this move, but she eventually agreed with her husband's way of thinking. She said, "Our son should have a career in music. ... I am thoroughly convinced: his bow has a voice."

Since Hiao-Tsiun's main instrument was the violin, he hastened to find the best cello teachers for his son. He wrote letters to many people regarding the young prodigy. He knew that meeting the right people would advance Yo-Yo's career.

One such meeting took place in Paris in 1962. While on a European tour, the world-famous violinist

New York City provided a wealth of opportunities for young Yo-Yo Ma to develop as a musician.

Isaac Stern found out about Yo-Yo. A violinmaker told Stern that he must hear this unbelievable young Chinese boy. Stern wrote: "So it was arranged that I would listen to him. ... The cello he played looked larger than he was. I was astonished, truly astonished." From that time on, Stern kept in touch with Yo-Yo.

One day in 1962, the Ma family received an important letter, one that would have an impact on Yo-Yo's future. The letter was from Hiao-Tsiun's brother, Hiao-Jone Ma, who had been living in the

Isaac Stern (1920–2001) was known for helping guide the careers of young musicians.

United States for several years. He wrote to say he had decided to leave Rochester, New York, and return to China. Hiao-Tsiun was opposed to the idea. He knew that this was not the time for his brother to return to their homeland. Communists still controlled China, and the country remained poverty-stricken. Hiao-Tsiun had to see his brother to convince him not to return to China. So he took his life's savings, packed up the family, and headed to Rochester.

The Mas arrived there on a cold day. Icy wind whipped off Lake Ontario. Rochester was nothing like Paris. The Mas stayed for a month, after which Hiao-Tsiun was finally able to convince his brother to remain in the United States. Then he turned to his next task—arranging for Yo-Yo to perform.

In Rochester, the 7-year-old prodigy gave his first American concert at Nazareth College with Yeou-Cheng accompanying him at the piano. Yo-Yo also played a Bach piece—*Suite Number Two for Unaccompanied Cello*. The concert was a rousing success.

No manuscript of Bach's cello suites exists in the composer's own hand. In fact, for many years the suites were lost. However, there are copies of the six cello suites believed to have been made by Bach's second wife, Anna Magdalena Bach.

Before returning to Paris, the Ma family stopped in New York City. This was a dream come true for Hiao-Tsiun. Once there, he took to the streets.

He walked around Manhattan, soaking up the noise, the smells, and the sights. He found himself standing in front of Carnegie Hall, the famous concert hall built by steel magnate Andrew Carnegie. Hiao-Tsiun longingly imagined the day when Yo-Yo would play there as a professional musician.

While they were in New York City, Yo-Yo and his sister gave two concerts in smaller settings. After the second concert, Dr. Ma received an unexpected job offer, a music teaching position at the Trent School in New York City. The job included conducting a children's orchestra at this private elementary school. He accepted. The Ma family returned to Paris, packed up all of their belongings—including a box of English language records—and moved to New York City to start a new life.

In time, the Mas adjusted quite well to life in their new city. Dr. Ma's teaching job left little time for anxiety. Nothing fazed Yo-Yo. Life in New York was more difficult for Yeou-Cheng and her mother. Marina missed her beloved Paris. Yeou-Cheng told a journalist many years later, "It was easier for him [Yo-Yo] because he was young, and because he was always a charming, extroverted kid. But I was really puzzled for a long time."

For Yo-Yo, New York was exciting. He studied

Yo-Yo Ma's sister, Yeou-Cheng, runs the Children's Orchestra Society, which was founded by their father in 1962. As executive director, she continues to promote the music education that was so dear to Hiao-Tsiun Ma. The society runs four youth orchestras, a chamber music program, and private lessons for gifted children. In addition to her duties there, Yeou-Cheng works as a pediatrician in New York City. Although not as well-known as her brother, she plays violin as a chamber musician.

Spanish musician Pablo Casals is considered the foremost cellist of the 20th century. A prodigy, he began his concert career before the turn of the century. His superb interpretations of the Bach unaccompanied cello suites brought him enormous fame. Casals believed strongly in freedom and human rights. Yo-Yo Ma said, "He saw himself not primarily as a cellist but as a musician, and even more as a member of the human race." At age 16, Ma played in an orchestra under the direction of Pablo Casals, who was 95 at the time.

hard at his new school and enjoyed learning English. Also, he began cello lessons with his first master teacher, the noted cellist Janos Scholz. "He proved to be the most extraordinary, the most charming and simple little boy imaginable," Scholz later recalled. "He was so eager to acquire musical knowledge that he just lapped it up."

Hiao-Tsiun's efforts to find a wider audience for his son led to a meeting with Pablo Casals, one of the greatest cellists of the 20th century. Instead of being awed by the great cellist, 7-year-old Yo-Yo sat down and played. And then he played some more. A grown-up Yo-Yo told a reporter that he did not remember what Casals said about his playing, "but he did suggest that I should be given more time to go and play in the street." An impressed Casals recommended that Leonard Bernstein include Yo-Yo on the program for a fund-raising concert in Washington, D.C.

The year 1964 was an important one for Yo-Yo's career. The young musician made his first appearance as a soloist with an orchestra. This meant that he sat

by himself in front of the orchestra and played his cello. Later that year, he and his sister were guests on *The Tonight Show* on television.

By this time, Hiao-Tsiun had accepted a job at the Ecole Française, a French school in Manhattan.

Pablo Casals (1876–1973) was considered to be one of the greatest musicians of his time.

33

Yo-Yo and Yeou-Cheng Ma listened to the advice of teacher Michelle LaPinte in 1964.

He took Yo-Yo with him. The Ecole Française was a good fit for both of them. Like Yo-Yo, many students had parents who participated in the arts. Many of the classes in the small school were taught in French, a language Yo-Yo spoke, so the school's atmosphere felt comfortable to him.

On December 17, 1964, the parents and students staged a fund-raiser for the school. This was no ordinary school auditorium event, however. The parents rented Carnegie Hall for the benefit concert, and *The New York Times* sent a reporter to cover it.

Virtuoso violinist Isaac Stern had a child at the school and was one of the many parents who performed. Hiao-Tsiun Ma directed the performance by the student orchestra. Then, Yo-Yo and his sister took the stage.

According to the newspaper reporter:

> *Yo-Yo Ma, the conductor's nine-year-old son, a cellist, then joined his twelve-year-old sister, Yeou-Cheng, to play Sammartini's G Major Cello Sonata. This is no children's piece, nor did they play like children. The performance had assurance, poise, and a full measure of delicate musicality.*

That night, the Mas left Carnegie Hall feeling overjoyed. For Hiao-Tsiun, Marina, and Yeou-Cheng, their new city had become home. For young Yo-Yo, performing on the stage of the world-famous concert hall had been just another day in his musical life. Little did he know that in just seven years, he would be back at Carnegie Hall, performing his first professional recital. ✑

4 GROWING PAINS

⟨⟨✕⟩⟩

Soon after his successful performance at the fundraiser, Yo-Yo Ma changed cello teachers. After two years of study with Janos Scholz, it was time to move on. Isaac Stern arranged for Yo-Yo to study with Leonard Rose at the Juilliard School of Music. At the time, Rose was considered to be the country's finest cello teacher. At Stern's recommendation, he gladly took Yo-Yo on as a new pupil.

Rose's teaching style was relaxed and informal, which was a marked change for Yo-Yo. His former teacher, Janos Scholz, had been very formal. During his first lessons, the usually outgoing Yo-Yo was so intimidated by Rose that he spoke in whispers and even tried to hide behind his cello. Yo-Yo recalled later that his teacher encouraged him to overcome his

New York City's Carnegie Hall is one of the nation's premier performance sites.

The Juilliard School in New York City has been preparing students for a life in the arts for more than 100 years. Established in 1905, it was then known as the Institute of Musical Art. In 1969, the school moved to the Lincoln Center for the Performing Arts and adopted its present name. Juilliard is widely considered the nation's finest arts school for music, dance, and drama, and has a long list of distinguished graduates.

timidity "by constantly urging me to sing out on the instrument." But as Stern recalled, "Lenny told me that ... Yo-Yo would come to every lesson perfectly prepared. ... He played every piece from memory. ... He bloomed under Lenny."

Beginning in 1964, student and teacher worked together with one goal in mind: a major New York recital. This was what Yo-Yo's father had imagined when he stood in front of Carnegie Hall on that first trip to New York City.

As Yo-Yo's music studies continued, so did school. Yo-Yo came to realize that he lived in two contradictory worlds. His Chinese heritage demanded strict obedience and discipline. Yet Americans valued freedom and self-expression. He said, "At home, I was to submerge my identity. You can't talk back to your parents—period. At school, I was expected to answer back, to reveal my individuality."

Schoolwork, music lessons, and language studies took up Yo-Yo's time. His busy schedule left no time for ballgames or parties or trips to the movies with friends. Marina explained:

We didn't allow our children to have too many friends or to participate in too many outside activities. ... In America, there are always so many goings on. ... My children had very little free time.

Leonard Rose (1918–1984) considered his student Yo-Yo Ma to be like a son.

By age 13, Yo-Yo was struggling to find his place. Looking back on those days, Yo-Yo recalled:

> *My home life was totally structured. Because I couldn't rebel there, I did so at school. In the fifth grade, I began to cut classes, and I continued doing so through high school. I spent a lot of time wandering through the streets, mainly because I just wanted to be alone.*

New York City's Juilliard School is a leading school for the performing arts.

In 1968, Yo-Yo enrolled at the Professional Children's School in New York City, a private school

for students who work in the arts. He missed so many classes that his teachers assumed he was bored, so they put him in a more difficult, accelerated program that would allow him to graduate early.

Toward the end of his high school studies, Yo-Yo's concert schedule grew heavier. When he was younger, his parents had limited his public appearances, wanting to avoid overexposure and overwork for their son. Now requests for Yo-Yo to perform kept coming.

In March 1971, he performed at Radcliffe College in Cambridge, Massachusetts. While he was there, he visited his sister Yeou-Cheng, who was enrolled as a biochemistry and music student. He also toured nearby Harvard University.

On May 6, 1971, Yo-Yo Ma reached a milestone in his musical journey: He gave his first professional recital, called a debut. It took place in New York's Carnegie Recital Hall, fulfilling his father's dream. Seven years of hard work—lesson after lesson— had paid off for Leonard Rose and his 15-year-old pupil. The review in *The New York Times* praised young Yo-Yo:

> *Yo-Yo Ma is said to have been a prodigy when he was a child, and although he is growing older now ... one can well believe it. The cello recital he gave at Carnegie Recital Hall on Thursday night was of a*

*quality to make many an older man green
with envy.*

After the recital, Rose decided it was time for
Yo-Yo to begin interpreting music for himself. In the
past, Rose had helped him understand a new piece
before playing it. Now Rose assigned his pupil a
piece by German composer Ludwig van Beethoven.
Yo-Yo was on his own to learn the C-Major Sonata

*Ludwig van
Beethoven
(1770–1827)
was a famous
and influential
composer of
classical music.*

without guidance. He later reflected, "One of the hardest things a teacher can do is to give a student permission to go his own way. I'll always be grateful to Mr. Rose for that."

In June 1971, one month after his Carnegie Hall debut, Yo-Yo completed high school. He was only 15 years old. That summer, he decided to attend Meadowmount, a camp for string players in New York's Adirondack Mountains. For the first time, he was away from home on his own. He felt totally free.

It was also the first time Yo-Yo had been with so many other young musicians. He spent much of that summer making new friends, playing Ping-Pong and cards, and talking until dawn. The other students adored him. Owen Carman, a fellow cellist who later became director of Meadowmount, recalled, "Everybody loved him, not only because he was so great, but because he was a wonderful kid."

Recalling the experiences of that summer, Yo-Yo said:

The Meadowmount School of Music, founded in 1944, is a seven-week summer school for talented young violinists, violists, cellists, and pianists training for professional careers in music. Students come from all parts of the United States and the world to this quiet mountain setting in New York state. Away from the hubbub of cities and towns, the students study, practice, and perform. Yo-Yo Ma is one of the school's many distinguished alumni.

*I had always kept my emotions bottled
up, but at Meadowmount I just ran wild,
as if I'd been let out of a ghetto. The
whole structure of discipline collapsed.
I exploded into bad taste at every level.*

*Meadowmount
School of Music
is located in
upstate New
York's beauti-
ful Adirondack
Mountains.*

This newfound sense of freedom showed in his behavior. Yo-Yo horrified the camp director by painting graffiti on the stone walls. Afterward, he spent a whole day washing it off. His other escapades included drinking beer, leaving his cello outside in the rain, and skipping rehearsals. No matter that he

did not practice much; he was more than ready for his performances.

Yo-Yo displayed his new sense of freedom in his playing, and his music-making became more creative. Fellow camper Wendy Rose, who later became a violinist in the Toronto Symphony, remembered her reaction to his solo concert: "I heard Yo-Yo playing the Franck sonata, and I burst into tears. The sheer beauty of his playing was totally overwhelming. I just couldn't stop crying."

Yo-Yo Ma remembers his experiences at Meadowmount as a turning point in his life. The cello had become his voice, and he had a lot to share. He later said, "I just started playing my heart out. You're 15. You've got a lot of feelings inside. From that moment on, it's been a continuing process."

Back in the city after a summer in the country, he found the stresses of his life mounting again. ❧

5 EXPANDING HORIZONS

Chapter

ecxxe

After Meadowmount, Yo-Yo Ma faced a critical time in his adolescence. He had played the cello since he was 4 years old, but now he began to doubt whether he wanted to become a professional musician. He was certain about one thing, however: He did not want to enroll full time in a music conservatory. Moreover, he realized he was not ready to leave home. He ended up spending the next year in New York City living with his parents. He enrolled at Columbia University and continued his musical studies with Leonard Rose at Juilliard.

In his efforts to be a typical teenager, Yo-Yo let his hair grow and wore a leather jacket. He spoke to Rose using language designed to shock. "But Mr. Rose took it in his stride and saw me through this

Yo-Yo Ma spent four summers playing—cello and otherwise—at Vermont's Marlboro Music Festival.

phase," Yo-Yo admitted years later. "All I was trying to do was to be accepted as one of the guys, and not be considered a freak."

Yo-Yo quickly grew bored at Columbia and felt that taking college courses was not much different from high school. Again, he lapsed into his old habit of cutting classes. Without telling his parents, he eventually dropped out of Columbia University, never completing a single semester.

For a time, Yo-Yo spent his days hanging out with the drinking crowd at Juilliard. Trying to act older than his age, he acquired a fake I.D in order to get alcohol. One day he drank so much that he passed out in a practice room at Juilliard and was taken by ambulance to a nearby hospital.

Some people regarded his misconduct as typical adolescent behavior, but his parents felt betrayed and ashamed by Yo-Yo's behavior. He stopped drinking after this embarrassing incident.

At age 16, Yo-Yo Ma had reached a crossroads. His options included becoming a professional musician or going back to college. He chose college, and this time decided to attend Harvard University. Isaac Stern recalled, "During those growing years—whatever growing pains there were—Yo-Yo made a decision rather remarkable for a talented young man of his age, and that was to try to get an education." By attending Harvard, Yo-Yo claimed, he would have the chance to simply experience life. He knew his playing would improve if he were able to understand more about the world.

Before entering Harvard, Yo-Yo spent the summer at the Marlboro Music Festival, which was attended by performers from all over the world. Here, in rural Marlboro, Vermont, Yo-Yo performed and learned from more experienced players. He played in the orchestra under the direction of Pablo Casals, then in his mid-90s. "I'll never forget the way his mind and body would radiate vitality the moment he raised his baton. That was an inspiration for a lifetime," Ma remembered.

Pablo Casals directed the Marlboro Festival Orchestra, of which Yo-Yo Ma was a member.

Yo-Yo would spend four summers at Marlboro and make many lasting friendships. One close relationship was with pianist Emanuel Ax, an acclaimed musician in his own right with whom Ma later formed a long-lasting musical partnership.

Yo-Yo formed another lasting relationship at Marlboro. During his first summer in 1972, he became friends with festival administrator Jill Hornor. She was attractive with dark, curly hair, and had just completed her sophomore year at Mount Holyoke, a woman's college near Boston. The two discovered they shared similar interests and backgrounds. Like Yo-Yo, Jill played a string instrument, the violin, and she had also been brought up in two cultures. She had lived in Europe for many years. Yo-Yo said, "But more important, she was probably the first person who really wanted to find out what I truly thought."

By the end of that summer, 16-year-old Yo-Yo was in love. In the fall, he entered Harvard University as a freshman, and Jill went to Paris

Harvard University is located in Cambridge, Massachusetts, just across the Charles River from Boston. The institution was founded in 1636 as Harvard College and is the oldest college in the United States. Graduates of Harvard University have gone on to make astounding discoveries in science, found large companies, and try important legal cases. A number of graduates have served as president of the United States, including John Adams, John Quincy Adams, Theodore Roosevelt, and Franklin Delano Roosevelt. Writers Henry David Thoreau and Ralph Waldo Emerson were also Harvard graduates.

Harvard University is the oldest college in the United States.

for her junior year. They stayed connected through daily letters and phone calls.

At college, Yo-Yo chose humanities as his major. He took courses in a wide variety of subjects, ranging from the history of civilizations to Russian literature. He later admitted that he managed to juggle his heavy schedule with his music performances because making perfect grades was not a top priority for him. He just wanted to learn as much as possible about as many things as possible.

Studying about people and other cultures stimulated his curiosity. His favorite subject was anthropology. "I wanted to try to tie together the various threads of my life—my Chinese upbringing, the atmosphere of Paris, my totally different experience in America," he explained. He learned about the Bushmen of the Kalahari Desert in Africa. Their culture fascinated him, and Yo-Yo made up his mind to visit the region some day. Studying anthropology helped him understand the variety of values in all cultures.

Yo-Yo also took many music courses at Harvard. Musically, he flourished there. His teachers recognized his immense talent and wanted to turn him into an even greater musician. They pushed him and challenged him. Moreover, they criticized his playing and taught him to analyze music in new ways. Isaac Stern said of Yo-Yo's experience at Harvard, "He learned musical analysis and a good deal about life in general. But, above all, he learned how to learn."

While at Harvard, Yo-Yo received numerous

requests to perform with professional orchestras. During his freshman year alone, he played 30 concerts all over the world. He had so many offers that he thought of leaving school, but his father insisted that he stay and limit his concerts to one a month.

Limiting his out-of-town concerts allowed Yo-Yo to become more involved in the social and musical life of Harvard. Whenever he performed on campus, students rushed to purchase tickets. The young cellist with the strange-sounding name was considered a phenomenon—and also a regular guy. One of his roommates, a pianist, remembered:

> *One of my enduring images is Yo-Yo inviting a crush of people, who couldn't get tickets, into the transept [lobby] of Memorial Hall at about 7:30 and playing Bach suites for them, right up to the moment he had to go on stage.*

Yo-Yo Ma's college years came to a close in 1976. He graduated from Harvard with a bachelor of arts degree in humanities. Then he embarked on a full-time career as a cellist. ℘

6 ON THE ROAD

❧❀❧

Offers to perform came pouring in after Yo-Yo Ma's graduation. Wanting to do everything, he found it hard to say no. Ma traveled constantly. From fall to spring, he performed with orchestras all over the United States and in Europe, playing as many as 150 concerts each season. Despite his grueling schedule, Ma said, "During my first years of performing, all the traveling and concertizing seemed terribly exciting. … [But] I was always flirting with getting burned out from exhaustion."

Even in the summers, Ma did not slow down. He played chamber music and taught at various music festivals, including the Spoleto Festival USA in Charleston, South Carolina; the Aspen Music Festival in Aspen, Colorado; and the Tanglewood Music

Yo-Yo Ma was 23 years old when he won the prestigious Avery Fisher Prize.

Festival in Lenox, Massachusetts.

Throughout his travels, Ma continued his long-distance relationship with Jill Hornor. After she finished Mount Holyoke, she did graduate work in German at Cornell University in Ithaca, New York. By the spring of 1977, Yo-Yo and Jill had been dating for almost five years. A friend of Ma's offered some advice about Jill: "If you don't do something, fish swim away."

Ma took the advice. He called Jill from New York City, telling her that he would call back at 7 P.M. She assured him she would be home. Then he bought a wedding ring and two tickets to Cleveland, Ohio, where Jill's parents lived. Attired in his best suit and tie, he took a bus to Ithaca. He rang Jill's doorbell— right on time. She answered the door, and before she could utter a word, he knelt and asked her to marry him. She accepted. Ma then said, "Good. Here's the ring and here are the tickets. We're going to see your parents."

On May 20, 1978, they were married. By marrying a non-Chinese girl, Ma broke from traditional Chinese culture. Initially, his parents were displeased. They had hoped their son would marry a Chinese woman and that his children would learn Chinese traditions. Eventually, however, tensions eased, and Jill was accepted into the Ma family.

The couple spent their first three years of married

life at Harvard, where Ma served as artist-in-residence. He gave concerts, taught master classes, and served as an adviser to music students who needed direction in their lives. Jill was a tutor in the German department

Yo-Yo Ma spent much of his early life on the East Coast of the United States.

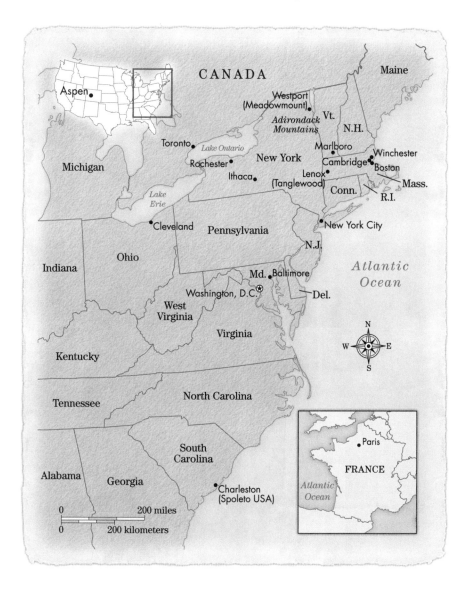

at Harvard. At first, the newlyweds planned to share the cooking and other household duties. However, Ma had little time to spend at home, and Jill was left with the responsibility of running the household.

In 1978, at age 23, Ma received the highest honor given in the United States to a musician: the Avery

Yo-Yo Ma and his wife, Jill Hornor, posed at a benefit in 2006.

Fisher Prize. The Lincoln Center in New York City awards the prize, which recognizes extremely talented young instrumentalists. Winning this highly esteemed prize advanced Ma's career. Soon orchestras all over the world wanted him to perform with them. More and more he was away from home—spending time on airplanes, in hotel rooms, and on stages. He returned home from his trips exhausted, and by the time the jet lag wore off, he was on the road again.

By April 1980, Ma had developed scoliosis, a serious medical condition in which the spine is curved. In Ma's case, his cello playing may have worsened the condition. Left untreated, the spinal condition could affect his internal organs, so surgery was required. Doctors warned that the risky operation could cause nerve damage, which could mean the end of his performance career. Before the surgery, Ma said, "Look, if I come out of this alive but not able to have total control of my fingers I will have had a very fulfilling life in music."

The operation was a success. Awakening after surgery, Ma wondered how many inches he had grown. In fact, he had gained 2 inches (5 centimeters). The taller Yo-Yo Ma remained in an upper body cast for six months. He joked, "With my cast on, I felt like a football player. I had broad shoulders, a fabulous physique."

After the cast came off, Ma resumed his exhausting

schedule. He played at least 120 concerts all over the world during the 1980–1981 season. Because he felt it was important to play new music, Ma began playing one or two new pieces written by contemporary composers in addition to his usual pieces.

During his travels, Ma found himself in an unusual situation. One afternoon, en route to a concert in Frankfurt, Germany, his car broke down along the highway. Motorists speeding by witnessed a strange sight alongside the road. Perched on top of his suitcase near the disabled car was Yo-Yo Ma, playing a cello. While waiting for help to arrive, he spent his time practicing.

Early in his professional career, Yo-Yo Ma performed more than 100 concerts a year.

In July 1981, Ma was once again at the Kennedy Center in Washington, D.C. First, he played a Beethoven sonata, accompanied on the piano by Emanuel Ax, his friend from his summers at Marlboro. Then he played the D-Major Cello Concerto by the 18th-century Austrian composer Franz Joseph Haydn. When he finished, the cheering audience gave him a standing ovation. Ma returned to the stage again and again for another bow. The enthusiastic scene was much the same as when Yo-Yo, at the age of 7, performed at the fund-raiser for the national arts center.

Emanuel Ax said:

> *A pianist could go on playing for 100 years and not begin to complete the standard repertoire. For a cellist, if you are a talent like Yo-Yo, by the time you are 25 you have mastered all the cello concertos that are known.*

Feeling limited by the number of pieces written for cello, Ma adapted pieces written for other instruments. He also expanded his repertoire by commissioning or requesting composers to write specifically for him.

Yo-Yo Ma did not slow down until 1983. By this time, the Mas had moved to Winchester, Massachusetts. However, Yo-Yo's hectic concert schedule left little time at home. "Then Nicholas was born," Ma told a reporter. "When you have your first child, everything changes. You realize ... that you absolutely have a limit to your energy." Nearly three years later, the Mas had a second child, a daughter they named Emily.

In 1983, Ma experienced changes in his professional life, too. He cut back on traveling by saying no to some concerts. He purchased a fine Italian cello made by Domenico Montagnana in 1733. His collection would eventually include a 1722 Matteo Goffriller and the renowned Davidoff Stradivarius made in 1712. Ma acquired the "Strad" following the death of its owner, renowned cellist Jacqueline du Pré. In addition to his older Italian cellos, Ma also plays modern cellos. Each of his instruments has a fine but different tone quality.

It was in 1983 that Ma launched his career as a recording artist. He recorded two of Beethoven's sonatas for cello and piano, with Emanuel Ax playing the piano. The same year, Ma also recorded his

Once in 1999, Yo-Yo Ma accidentally left his famed Montagnana cello in the trunk of a New York City taxicab. Luckily, Ma had kept the receipt. It took only a few hours for the police to track down the cab and driver. The cello, valued at $2.5 million, was returned to Ma in time for his evening concert. Happy to be reunited with his 266-year-old cello, Ma said, "The instrument is my voice, so I need it." The incident made headline news. For a long time afterward, everybody greeted the cellist with, "Been in a taxi lately?"

Emanuel Ax has been Ma's friend and musical collaborator since their summers together at Marlboro.

favorite music—the Bach cello suites. In 1984, the album won Ma his first Grammy, the major award for outstanding achievement in the recording industry. Less than 15 years later, he would record the Bach suites again. In the meantime, however, Ma embarked on a series of journeys that would stretch musical boundaries in entirely new directions. ❧

7 STRETCHING MUSICAL BOUNDARIES

❧

For 15 years after graduating from college, Yo-Yo Ma followed a typical classical concert and recording career. But in 1991, he began to pursue more wide-ranging musical interests, including new ways to make music. That year he went high-tech and worked on a project that combined a Bach piece with modern technology. He premiered a piece of electronic music composed by Tod Machover, a professor at Massachusetts Institute of Technology. Ma played Bach's Second Cello Suite on an electric cello. Rigged with sensors, the hypercello hooked into four computers. Reviewers found Machover's music strange, describing it as alternately shrieking and purring.

In another project, Ma worked with jazz singer

Yo-Yo Ma plays Bach's First Cello Suite in a scene from the film series Yo-Yo Ma: Inspired by Bach.

65 ↝

Bobby McFerrin, well-known for his hit song "Don't Worry, Be Happy." The pairing of a singer with a cellist might seem odd; however, they shared a lot in common—most of all musical curiosity. Like Ma, the jazz vocalist grew up surrounded by classical music. When they met, both were going through periods of change. Ma wanted to play jazz; McFerrin wanted to return to his classical musical roots.

McFerrin's singing style is unique. He sings not only the words but also their musical accompaniments, using his voice to imitate the instruments in a jazz band. McFerrin taught Ma how to improvise, or make up, some of the music during a performance. In time, the duo found a way to mesh their musical styles. In 1992, they recorded an album called *Hush*, which combines McFerrin's distinctive singing style with Ma's classical cello playing. It was billed as a crossover album, a recording made by a musician who "crosses over" from his or her field of music to join other musicians in a different field. The album was a hit, and the experience of creating it whetted Ma's appetite for more musical experiments.

In 1993, an old dream of Ma's came true. As a student at Harvard, he had heard the music of the Kalahari Bushmen on tape in his anthropology class. The sounds had haunted him ever since. Now he struck out on a personal quest to learn about the music of Africa's Kalahari Desert.

After arriving in Africa, Ma set off for the Bushmen villages in the African nation of Namibia. A guide/translator and a film crew accompanied him. Ma's plans for the trip included making a documentary, called *Distant Echoes*.

Bobby McFerrin is a unique vocalist who often uses his voice to imitate other instruments.

The Bushmen have made the Kalahari Desert their home for a very long time. Evidence indicates

The Kalahari Desert in Africa covers a vast region within the countries of Namibia, Botswana, and South Africa. Covered largely by reddish sand, the Kalahari is studded with dry lake beds. There is no permanent surface water. Some parts support low thorn scrub and grasses. Animals that live in the region include antelope, hyenas, lions, and many species of bird and reptile. One of the largest diamond mines in the world is located in the northeastern Kalahari. This area is the home-land of the nomadic Bushmen tribes.

they have lived in the same area continuously for at least 20,000 years. Until recently, life for these nomadic hunter-gatherers remained unchanged. In the midst of this ancient culture, Ma performed for a group of local musicians. He played Bach on his cello. The villagers showed little interest in listening to him. "They said, 'Stop. Don't play. We want to play for you,'" Ma remembers.

Fascinated by their music, Ma inquired, through an interpreter, about their instruments. Made of debris such as twigs and tin cans, they looked so simple. However, Ma discovered that playing them was not easy. He tried to play one of the instruments, a *venturo*, which was basically an oil can with a metal string and a wooden bow. His struggle with the venturo gave everyone a big laugh.

The experiences Ma had in the Kalahari Desert have affected his musical career ever since. He said he learned that the role of a musician is not only "[t]o uphold cultural memory—but also to innovate." He

decided, from then on, to learn to play many different kinds of music. And so he has.

On his return to the United States, Ma became

The Bushmen of the Kalahari have intrigued Ma since his college days.

69

interested in Appalachian fiddle music. The Appalachian mountain range, which extends from Canada to Georgia, is home to a type of folk music that features the fiddle. Early settlers to this region came from England, Ireland, and Scotland and brought their distinctive fiddling traditions with them.

It took a year of coaching and hours of practice for Ma to learn how to play fiddle music on his cello. His teachers were fiddler Mark O'Connor and bassist Edgar Meyer. In a *New York Times* article, O'Connor recalled:

> *Yo-Yo said that whatever we did, he wanted to be stretched. So we came up with some really good fiddle material that we hoped would challenge him. It was amazing to see him process this intellectually and make it work on his instrument. It has been quite a transformation.*

In 1996, the trio recorded *Appalachia Waltz*. The album contains traditional American songs, as well as new music written by O'Connor and Meyer. It was a tremendous success. On tour to promote the album, the three musicians played to packed concert halls at every stop. The album's sequel, *Appalachian Journey*, won a Grammy for Best Classical Crossover Album of 2000.

During his explorations of American folk music,

Ma began looking to South America for inspiration. In 1997, his search for new kinds of music to play took him to Buenos Aires, the capital of Argentina. Here he investigated the music of the tango, a dance native to that country. In the later half of the 19th century, immigrants to Argentina from Italy and

Spain filled the countryside. They brought with them a *bandoneon,* an accordionlike instrument. Soon the bandoneon became the central instrument in tango music.

Ma found the tango music of 20th-century Argentine composer Astor Piazzolla intriguing. Piazzolla fused elements of classical music and

Astor Piazzolla (1921–1992) began his musical career playing the bandoneon in nightclubs.

jazz with traditional Argentine tango music. The composer also included the cello in his arrangements. This new music was more for listening than for dancing. Argentine musicians joined Ma in the recording of Piazzolla's music. The album was called *Soul of the Tango—The Music of Astor Piazzolla*, and it won a Grammy Award for Best Classical Crossover Album in 1998.

Yo-Yo Ma's many awards reflect the extent of his musical styles, which range from classical music to jazz, Appalachian, and tango music. His extraordinary achievements show that the boundaries of classical music need not be restraining.

> *Argentine tango music inspired the tango dance. The dance spread to Europe early in the 20th century and then to the United States. The unique dance consists of slow steps, sudden turns, and dramatic poses. The tango craze peaked during the 1920s, but people still dance the tango today. The dance is popular with professional dance troupes and ballroom dancers.*

At times, Ma has wandered far from classical music, but he has never left it completely. The music of Johann Sebastian Bach has always been a part of Yo-Yo Ma's life. At age 4, he inch-wormed his way through the suites for unaccompanied cello and has continued to perform the suites throughout his career. His performances of these pieces involve nothing but a chair and cellist on a bare concert stage. Ma recorded the six suites soon after he became a

The Bach cello suites are most often performed by a cellist alone on stage.

professional musician.

In 1991, Ma's father suffered a severe stroke. Before he died on August 28, 1991, he made a request of his son: Play Bach. Yo-Yo played the Sarabande from Bach's *Fifth Suite for Unaccompanied Cello* at Hiao-Tsiun Ma's deathbed.

In the mid-1990s, Yo-Yo Ma began a new musical journey. In this venture, he returned to Bach's six cello suites for an unusual experiment. Ma wondered how artists from other fields would interpret the six suites. "I wanted to know what would an actor, a filmmaker, a dancer do with a piece of music," said Ma. And so the project was born. For this new project, Ma recorded the Bach suites again, only the new version included visual interpretations of the music.

The six films that make up *Yo-Yo Ma: Inspired by Bach* were six years in the making. They explore the relationship between music and other art forms, such as architecture, dance, and theater, and showcase such varied additional performers as Jayne Torvill and Christopher Dean, a pair of world-champion ice skaters, and Tamasaburo Bando, a traditional Japanese kabuki actor. The films, released in 1998, received mixed reviews. Still, for Ma, making the films provided "new ways of thinking and approaching something. It made me an infinitely richer person, and I think a better musician." ℘

Doctor, minister, and Bach expert Albert Schweitzer (1875–1965) was the inspiration for Ma's film interpretations of Bach's suites for unaccompanied cello. Schweitzer believed the music of Bach created images in the mind of the listener; he compared Bach to a painter who uses sound to create pictures. This idea intrigued Ma, who decided to work with artists in other fields to create visual interpretations of Bach's famous suites.

8 MAKING CONNECTIONS

⸉⸜⸝⸌⸍

Yo-Yo Ma's films used music to connect ideas, but for Ma, music's real power is in connecting people. He believes that "music can act as a magnet to draw people together." While growing up, Yo-Yo was fortunate to connect with and receive guidance from many adults. His father, violinist Isaac Stern, and cello teacher Leonard Rose all nurtured him as a musician and person. As an adult, Ma seeks out opportunities to help the next generation of musicians.

Like his father, Ma enjoys teaching. Much of his teaching takes place at the Tanglewood Music Festival. There he coaches chamber groups, performs with Tanglewood's Youth Orchestra, and counsels students on the ins and outs of the music business. He encourages them to take the time to develop both

Ma worked with a student orchestra in Tel Aviv, Israel, in 2006.

The Tanglewood Music Festival, located in the Berkshire Mountains of Massachusetts, began in 1937. Tanglewood is the summer home for the Boston Symphony Orchestra. The music festival is one of the most famous in the United States. More than 350,000 people attend the summer-long festival each year, to take in the concerts and enjoy the beautiful countryside.

as musicians and as people. He discourages them from focusing too heavily on performing, saying:

I believe the years between 15 and 20-something are crucial to your development; everything you learn during that time is a reserve to draw on. If you put all your energy into performing instead of opening yourself to experimenting and discovering new ways of making music, you'll be a diminished person. You may never have another opportunity to explore, find the depth of your own soul and other people's, and isn't that what music is all about?

Ma also teaches master classes, which allow him to share his wisdom and to interact with young people. Just as master classes at Juilliard, Meadowmount, and Marlboro influenced Ma's development as an artist, he hopes that his master classes will do the same for his students. He says:

[I] just take them through what the thinking process is, how you deal with the hall as an instrument, how you make it friendly, how you think of a release [from a note], or what questions they have.

Ma performs chamber music with violinists Itzhak Perlman (left) and Midori.

In a typical master class, Ma teaches a small group of young performers. He listens as each student performs and then offers his feedback on the student's playing. After that, Ma demonstrates how to correctly play the piece. At these group events, everyone in the room hears the other performers. They also listen to Ma's remarks and demonstrations.

When Ma offers advice to young musicians, he uses terms that are understandable to them. For example, in a master class in Minneapolis, Minnesota,

In 2000, Ma taught master classes at the World Cello Congress at Towson State University near Baltimore, Maryland. The event brought together 600 musicians from 45 countries. He began his instruction with an event called a "children's cello party." Eight children ranging in age from 7 to 12 attended the class, which was closed to the public. After the event, a conductor associated with some of the children said that they had moved to a whole new level of performance as a result of Ma's instruction.

he told an 11-year-old boy how to get a fuller sound from his cello. He suggested that the student push his bow and really follow through with it, as if he were throwing a ball.

Ma finds other ways to connect with young people as well. He uses television as a means of introducing classical music to very young children. After all, he made his first appearance on television when he was 7 years old. Ma has appeared on *Sesame Street* and *Mister Rogers' Neighborhood*. He performed a cello-violin duet with Elmo on *Sesame Street*. Remembering the experience, Ma said, "I am very proud that I knew Elmo before he became a superstar." He was proud of the work he did on the two television programs, and he later told a journalist that his appearances were some of the most important things he'd ever done.

In 1999, Ma appeared as a guest on the children's show *Arthur*. Through animation, he was portrayed as a giant bunny with flapping ears and glasses clutching his cello.

Soon after, Ma—in human form—made a video for young musicians called *Tackling the Monster*. He and trumpet player Wynton Marsalis discuss musical forms and the importance of practice. Ma advises students to find ways to connect their music-making with other things in their lives.

In the 1990s, Ma discovered other ways to connect to audiences: He played on the soundtracks of movies and television shows. His first soundtrack was for the film *Immortal Beloved* (1994), which

Trumpeter Wynton Marsalis is a successful crossover artist with best-selling albums in both jazz and classical styles.

tells the story of the life of composer Ludwig van Beethoven. The television miniseries *Liberty!: The American Revolution* (1997) came next. Ma joined the project because his fiddler friend Mark O'Connor wrote the score. Trumpeter Wynton Marsalis joined Ma again to play on the soundtrack.

Ma's two biggest commercial film projects have had Asian story lines. In 1997, he played on the soundtrack for *Seven Years in Tibet*. The composer John Williams wrote the Asian-influenced score. Ma enjoyed the challenge of Williams' music. Work on this film prepared him for his next movie project,

The musical styles of Ma's crossover recordings span the globe.

an even grander Asian tale.

In 2000, Ma performed on the soundtrack for the movie *Crouching Tiger, Hidden Dragon*. This project fulfilled his desire to break down musical boundaries. It also allowed him to revisit his Chinese roots. Tan Dun, a native of China, composed the music, which called for both Chinese and Western instruments. The soundtrack won the Academy Award for Best Original Score. Accepting the Oscar, Tan Dun said, "My music is to dream without boundaries. Tonight with you, I see boundaries being crossed." He thanked the people who helped make the successful film. Special thanks went to Yo-Yo Ma.

9 TRAVELING THE SILK ROAD

☙❧

Touring the globe as a performer for 25 years, Yo-Yo Ma has traveled many fascinating musical roads. "Throughout my travels," Ma says, "I have thought about the culture, religions, and ideas ... and have wondered how these interconnections occurred." With the founding of the Silk Road Project in 1998, Ma began what is perhaps his most exciting musical journey so far.

Long ago the Silk Road linked Eastern and Western cultures. The Silk Road was not a single road, but a vast network of ancient trade routes that stretched for thousands of miles between China and the Mediterranean Sea. This historic network linked Asia and Europe from about 200 B.C. to A.D. 1500 and allowed merchants from both continents to trade silk and other items, such as horses, spices, tea, and gold. The ancient route connected people from all walks of life across great distances, allowing ideas, culture, and artistic forms to flow back and forth. Today the route that brought Italian explorer Marco Polo to China in the 13th century has become a symbolic path for fostering understanding between cultures.

Ma's vision for the Silk Road Project grew out of the age-old notion of music as a common language. He set out to examine the music of the Silk Road and foster cultural exchanges between these lands and the West through concerts, festivals, recordings, and educational outreach. "I believe that when we enlarge our view of the world we deepen our understanding of our own lives," Ma says, adding that the project is another step to "bring together musicians … to see how we can connect with each other."

During the project's planning phase, Ma invited scholars, musicians, and business people to attend worldwide conferences in Massachusetts, Paris, and

A historical illustration depicts valuable goods being shipped from Asia to Europe via the Silk Road.

Amsterdam. In time, these experts formed the Silk Road Project, a nonprofit organization.

In 1999, Ma named Theodore Levin, a Central Asia specialist who had studied and traveled the region for decades, to head the project. Just exploring the region's musical past was not enough for Ma. He had much bigger plans. He sent Levin to Uzbekistan, Kazakhstan, Mongolia, and other Central Asian countries to seek out native composers. Levin returned to the United States with sample works from 40 composers. A review panel selected 16 out of the 40 to work for the Silk Road Project,

Bright Sheng, Ma's Chinese-American composer and friend, served as an adviser on China for the Silk Road Project. In the summer of 2000, Sheng traveled 10,000 miles (16,000 km) along the Chinese part of the Silk Road. He interviewed residents and taped their music. He discovered that American pop culture reached almost every corner of the remote area and reported that traditional Chinese music was in danger of extinction as older generations died off. He urged the Silk Road Project to celebrate traditional Chinese music and native performers.

commissioning a new piece from each selected composer.

In July 2000, the Silk Road composers along with 42 other musicians gathered to rehearse at the Tanglewood Music Center in Lenox, Massachusetts. As they stepped off the bus, Ma was there to greet each one with a handshake or a hug. The next phase of the project—preparing for performance—had begun.

Although most of the musicians attending the 12-day workshop were Asian, they came from very different backgrounds. Their instruments were just as varied, ranging from members of the flute family to bowed and percussion instruments. Ma learned to play a *morin khuur*—a Mongolian version of the cello. Also called a horsehead fiddle, the bowed instrument has two strings and features a carving of a horse's head at the top of the neck. The cellist joked about his surname, Ma, meaning "horse."

Following the workshop, Ma formed the Silk Road Ensemble, a group made up of musicians

Ma posed with members of the Silk Road Ensemble.

from around the world. In August 2001, Ma and the Silk Road Ensemble made their first tour abroad. The 2001–2002 tour was a cooperative effort of the Silk Road Project and partner cities. The first stop was the weeklong Schleswig-Holstein Music Festival in Germany.

Following the appearance in Germany, two events occurred merely days apart that affected Ma deeply. On September 11, 2001, terrorists flew planes into the World Trade Center in New York City and the Pentagon in Washington, D.C. and crashed

In 2001, Yo-Yo Ma was awarded the National Medal of the Arts, the highest honor given to an artist by the U.S. government. Considered a lifetime achievement award, the recognition was especially significant because Ma was only 46 years old. At the awards ceremony, he performed the slow movement of Johannes Brahms' Violin Sonata in D minor in an arrangement for cello and piano. National Security Adviser Condoleezza Rice, a classically trained pianist, accompanied him on piano.

another into a Pennsylvania field. Thousands of innocent people lost their lives. Then on September 22, Isaac Stern, Ma's mentor and friend, died of a heart attack at age 81. Stern had heard Yo-Yo play when he was a little boy in Paris, and since that time, the two musicians had played together on stages around the globe.

On September 30, Ma performed twice in New York City. In the morning, he played at a memorial service for Isaac Stern. In the afternoon he joined other artists on the stage of Carnegie Hall for a free concert honoring the victims of the terrorist attacks.

Security concerns forced the Silk Road Ensemble to cancel its fall tour to Central Asia. However, the tour continued with stops in Washington D.C., and in Japan. In April 2002, the Silk Road Ensemble performed in Europe.

Silk Road Journeys: When Strangers Meet is the first recording of the Silk Road Ensemble. The album, which was released in 2002, includes Mongolian, Persian, and Chinese music. One of the many instruments played on the album is the morin khuur.

Following the recording, the Silk Road Project

A Mongolian musician performs on the traditional morin khuur.

continued its worldwide activities. In 2003, the Silk Road Ensemble finally toured Central Asia. Much of the music played by the group came from that region. They performed in Kazakhstan, Kyrgyzstan, and Tajikistan. While there, Ma taught master classes to young people. He even played with a local rock band in Kazakhstan.

While juggling his concert performances with the Silk Road Project, Ma still found time to explore different kinds of music. In 2003, he returned to South America. Brazilian music had grabbed his attention as a teenager. Now in Brazil, he rejoined many of the musicians from the tango project. Together, they recorded an album called *Obrigado Brazil*, which means "Thank you Brazil" in Portuguese. In the summer and fall of 2003, Ma and the musicians toured in support of the album, which won Ma another Grammy for Best Crossover Album and brought his total number of Grammy Awards to 15.

In 2004, Ma and the Silk Road Project reached beyond music to establish partnerships with museums in Asia, Europe, and North America. The museums showcased the art and architecture that developed along the historic route and offered performances, lectures, and workshops in regional craft making and storytelling. And in March 2005, the Silk Road Project teamed up with Harvard University and the Rhode Island School of Design to provide

Ma posed with an album cover of a 2004 classical recording.

cross-cultural learning experiences for students in both institutions. Ma is pleased with the evolution of the project, never having dreamed that it would expand in such exciting new directions.

In 2006, Yo-Yo Ma received the $1 million Dan David Prize from Tel Aviv University in Israel. The prize was awarded to him in recognition of his Silk Road Project and its contributions to international cultural understanding. In his acceptance speech, Ma said that he would share the money with the project's musicians, board members, and staff.

Yo-Yo Ma also won Denmark's 2006 Sonning Music Prize, an $80,000 award, for his contributions to world culture. This annual prize honors an internationally known composer, musician, conductor, or singer.

In his continued efforts to bring people together, Yo-Yo Ma launched a new project, called Silk Road Chicago, in 2006. For the first time, the art and culture of the historic Silk Road would be featured in one city throughout the year, beginning in June 2006 and ending in June 2007. More than 250 events for all ages were planned.

In 2006, 50-year-old Yo-Yo Ma took on a fitting new role as a United Nations peace ambassador. In this position, Ma took his communication skills out of the realm of music to travel around the world delivering a message of peace.

Over the course of his 25-year career, Yo-Yo Ma has become a musical superstar. He mastered the classical cello repertoire and kept on going in search of new types of music and new ways to communicate. Ma is a cellist, but the cello is not his message—it is his voice. He reflected on his career and his mission:

> *I play an instrument that has four strings,*
> *and I'm still trying to get it right. What*
> *I've tried to do in the process of playing*
> *these strings is to try and understand the*

people I meet, the stories they have to tell. And then become an advocate for them and their stories through music. 🕭

Today Ma makes connections as a U.N. peace ambassador.

YO-YO MA'S LIFE

1955
Born October 7
in Paris, France

1959
Begins playing cello

1961
Performs first public
recital, playing cello
and piano

1960

1953
Sir Edmund Hillary
of New Zealand and
Tenzing Norgay of Nepal
are the first two men
to reach the summit of
Mount Everest

1959
The plane transporting
Buddy Holly, Ritchie
Valens, and the Big
Bopper goes down in an
Iowa snowstorm, killing
everyone on board; the
tragedy is later termed
the "day the music died"
in the song American Pie

1961
Soviet cosmonaut
Yuri Gagarin is
the first human to
enter space

WORLD EVENTS

1964

Studies with Leonard Rose at Juilliard School of Music; appears at Carnegie Hall and on *The Tonight Show* with his sister

1962

Ma family moves to New York City; Yo-Yo plays cello, accompanied by his sister on piano, at a fund-raising concert in Washington, D.C.

1971

Graduates from high school at age 15; attends summer camp for string players in New York's Adirondack Mountains

1965

1966

The National Organization for Women (NOW) is established to work for equality between women and men

1963

Dr. Michael De Bakey first uses an artificial heart to take over a person's circulation during heart surgery

1973

Spanish artist Pablo Picasso dies

Yo-Yo Ma's Life

1978

Marries Jill Hornor; wins Avery Fisher Prize

1976

Graduates from Harvard University

1980

Undergoes successful spine operation

1980

1981

Sandra Day O'Connor becomes the first woman on the U.S. Supreme Court

1975

Bill Gates and Paul Allen found Microsoft, which will become the world's largest software company

1979

The Soviet Union invades Afghanistan

World Events

1984

Wins first Grammy Award for *Bach: The Unaccompanied Cello Suites*

1983

Son Nicholas is born

1985

Daughter Emily is born

1984

U.S. scientists isolate the virus that causes AIDS (acquired immune deficiency syndrome), which will become a worldwide epidemic

1986

The U.S. space shuttle *Challenger* explodes, killing all seven astronauts on board

1985

Associated Press newsman Terry Anderson and others are taken hostage in Beirut, Lebanon; they are released in 1991

YO-YO MA'S LIFE

2000

Wins Grammy Award for *Appalachian Journey;* plays on soundtrack for movie, *Crouching Tiger, Hidden Dragon*

1998

Founds the Silk Road Project

1993

Visits the Kalahari Desert in Africa

1990

1991

The Soviet Union collapses and is replaced by the Commonwealth of Independent States

1997

At 14 years old, Tara Lipinski becomes the youngest skater to win the U.S. and world women's figure skating championships; the following year she becomes the youngest skater to win gold at the Olympics

2000

Draft of the human genome is completed

WORLD EVENTS

2001

Receives the National
Medal of the Arts,
the highest honor for
artistic excellence in
the United States

2003

Records *Obrigado
Brazil*

2006

Receives $1 million
Dan David Prize
and Denmark's 2006
Sonning Music Prize;
becomes U.N. peace
ambassador

2005

2001

Terrorist attacks on
the two World Trade
Center Towers in
New York City and
on the Pentagon in
Washington, D.C.,
leave thousands dead

2003

Heat wave scorches
Europe; more than
35,000 people die

2005

Pope John Paul II
dies; Joseph Ratzinger
of Germany is elected
Pope Benedict XVI

DATE OF BIRTH: October 7, 1955

BIRTHPLACE: Paris, France

FATHER: Hiao-Tsiun Ma
(1911–1991)

MOTHER: Marina Ma (Ya-Wen Lo)
(1923–)

EDUCATION: Bachelor's degree from
Harvard University

SPOUSE: Jill Hornor

**DATE OF
MARRIAGE:** May 20, 1978

CHILDREN: Nicholas (1983–)

Emily (1985–)

FURTHER READING

Ardley, Neil. *A Young Person's Guide to Music.* New York: Dorling Kindersley, 1995.

Chippendale, Lisa A. *Yo-Yo Ma: A Cello Superstar Brings Music to the World.* Berkeley Heights, N.J.: Enslow Publishers, 2004.

Kallen, Stuart A. *The History of Classical Music.* San Diego: Lucent Books, 2003.

Olmstead, Mary. *Yo-Yo Ma.* Chicago: Raintree, 2006.

Vernon, Roland. *Introducing Bach.* Philadelphia: Chelsea House, 2001.

LOOK FOR MORE SIGNATURE LIVES
BOOKS ABOUT THIS ERA:

Clara Barton: *Founder of the American Red Cross*

George Washington Carver: *Scientist, Inventor, and Teacher*

Amelia Earhart: *Legendary Aviator*

Thomas Alva Edison: *Great American Inventor*

Thurgood Marshall: *Civil Rights Lawyer and Supreme Court Justice*

Annie Oakley: *American Sharpshooter*

Will Rogers: *Cowboy, Comedian, and Commentator*

Amy Tan: *Writer and Storyteller*

Madam C.J. Walker: *Entrepreneur and Millionaire*

Booker T. Washington: *Innovative Educator*

On the Web

For more information on this topic,
use FactHound.

1. Go to *www.facthound.com*
2. Type in this book ID: 0756518792
3. Click on the *Fetch It* button.

FactHound will find the best
Web sites for you.

Historic Sites

Carnegie Hall
57th Street and 7th Avenue
New York, NY 10019
212/247-7800
Historic hall is one of the world's most
important venues for the performing arts

National Music Museum
414 E. Clark St.
Vermillion, SD 57069
605/677-5308
Collections of more than 10,000
instruments from all cultures and
historical periods

anthropology
the study of people, especially the aspects of
human development and culture

communists
people who believe that a government should own
most of the property and control the economy

conservatory
advanced music or drama school

improvise
to make something up on the spot, such as a piece
of music

intrigued
greatly interested or curious

physique
the size and shape of a person's body

prodigy
highly gifted young person

repertoire
supply of known musical or dramatic works that
can be performed

sequel
something that happens after something else, such
as a continuing story or musical work

suite
musical work that consist of several related but
different compositions

virtuosi
people who are highly talented in an area, such
as music

Chapter 1

Page 9, line 14: Marina Ma as told to John A. Rallo. *My Son, Yo-Yo.* Hong Kong: The Chinese University Press, 1995, pp. 81–82.

Page 13, line 2: John Attanos. *Yo-Yo Ma: A Life in Music.* Evanston, Ill.: John Gordon Burke Publisher, Inc., 2003, p. 21.

Page 13, sidebar: "About the Kennedy Center: History of the Living Memorial." 30 Oct. 2006, www.kennedy-center.org/about/chairmen.html

Page 14, line 9: *My Son, Yo-Yo,* p. 83.

Page 15, line 14: Andrew L. Pincus. *Musicians with a Mission.* Boston: Northeastern University Press, 2002, p. 5.

Chapter 2

Page 22, line 17: *My Son, Yo-Yo,* p. 28.

Page 23, line 3: Ibid., p. 29.

Chapter 3

Page 27, line 7: Ibid., p. 35.

Page 28, line 3: Isaac Stern. *My First 79 Years.* New York: Alfred A. Knopf, 1999, p. 166.

Page 31, line 24: *Yo-Yo Ma: A Life in Music,* p. 19.

Page 32, line 5: Claude Kenneson. *Musical Prodigies: Perilous Journeys, Remarkable Lives.* Portland, Ore.: Amadeus Press, 1998, p. 328.

Page 32, sidebar: David Blum. *Quintet: Five Journeys Toward Musical Fulfillment.* Ithaca, N.Y.: Cornell University Press, 1998, p. 6.

Page 32, line 21: *Musicians with a Mission,* p. 17.

Page 35, line 13: *Yo-Yo Ma: A Life in Music,* p. 23.

Chapter 4

Page 38, line 1: *Quintet: Five Journeys Toward Musical Fulfillment,* p. 10.

Page 38, line 3: Ibid.

Page 38, line 21: Ibid.

Page 39, line 1: *My Son, Yo-Yo,* p. 104.

Page 40, line 3: *Quintet: Five Journeys Toward Musical Fulfillment,* p. 11.

Page 41, line 24: *Yo-Yo Ma: A Life in Music,* p. 28.

Page 43, line 1: *Quintet: Five Journeys Toward Musical Fulfillment,* p. 12.

Page 43, line 24: *Yo-Yo Ma: A Life in Music,* p. 31.

Page 44, line 1: *Quintet: Five Journeys Toward Musical Fulfillment,* p. 11.

Page 45, line 7: Gerri Hirshey. "We Are the World." *Parade.* 30 Jan. 2005, www.parade.com/articles/editions/2005/edition_01-30-2005/featured_0

Page 45, line 14: Ibid.

Chapter 5

Page 47, line 14: *Musical Prodigies,* p. 329.

Page 48, line 24: *Quintet: Five Journeys Toward Musical Fulfillment,* pp. 13–14.

Page 49, line 10: Ibid.

Page 50, line 21: Janet Tassel. "Yo-Yo Ma's Journeys." *Harvard Magazine.* March–April 2000. 30 Oct. 2006. www.harvardmagazine.com/on-line/ 0300127.html

Page 52, line 1: *Quintet: Five Journeys Toward Musical Fulfillment*, p. 14.

Page 52, sidebar: "Yo-Yo Ma's Journeys."

Page 52, line 24: *Quintet: Five Journeys Toward Musical Fulfillment*, p. 17.

Page 53, line 13: *Yo-Yo Ma: A Life in Music*, p. 39.

Chapter 6

Page 55, line 7: *Quintet: Five Journeys Toward Musical Fulfillment*, p. 20.

Page 56, line 8: Ibid., p. 18.

Page 56, line 18: Ibid., p. 19.

Page 59, line 18: Ibid., p. 21.

Page 59, line 25: Ibid.

Page 61, line 14: Bruce Handy and Daniel S. Levy. "Yo-Yo Ma's Suite Life." *Time.* 23 March 1998.

Page 62, line 1: *Quintet: Five Journeys Toward Musical Fulfillment*, p. 20.

Page 62, sidebar: "Yo-Yo Ma's Cello Lost, Found." *Los Angeles Times.* 17 Oct. 1999.

Chapter 7

Page 68, line 10: Justin Davidson. "Have Cello, Will Travel." *Newsday.* 30 Nov. 1997, p. 1.

Page 68, line 27: Matthew Gurewitsch. "Master Ma." *Town & Country.* February 1998, p. 49.

Page 70, line 12: *Musicians with a Mission*, p. 20.

Page 74, line 11: Bonnie Churchill. "Music: 'Inspired' Idea." *Boston Herald.* 29 March 1998, p. 1.

Page 75, line 21: Edith Eisler. "Continuity in Diversity." *Strings.* 1 May 2001, p. 49.

Chapter 8

Page 77, line 3: *Musicians with a Mission*, p. 6.

Page 78, line 4: Edith Eisler. "Yo-Yo Ma as Experimenter, Colleague and Teacher." *andante.* May 2001. 30 Oct. 2006. www.andante.com/article/print. cfm?id=12748&varticletype=INTER

Page 78, line 26: *Musicians with a Mission*, p. 13.

Page 80, line 17: *Yo-Yo Ma: A Life in Music*, p. 81.

Page 83, line 10: Ibid., p. 124.

Chapter 9

Page 85, line 3: Susan Osmond. "Yo-Yo Ma's Silk Road Project." *World and I.* April 2002, p. 72.

Page 86, line 20: "A Journey of Discovery." *Program Book.* 2002 Smithsonian Folklife Festival. 30 Oct. 2006, www.silkroadproject.org/smithsonian

Page 94, line 25: Miriam Di Nunzio. "Yo-Yo Ma to Help Turn City Into Silk

Applebaum, Samuel and Sada. *The Way They Play*. Neptune City, N.J.: Paganiniana Publications, Inc., 1972.

Attanos, John. *Yo-Yo Ma: A Life in Music*. Evanston, Ill.: John Gordon Burke Publisher, Inc., 2003.

Bonavia, Judy. *The Silk Road*. New York: W.W. Norton & Company, Inc., 2002.

Blum, David. *Quintet: Five Journeys Toward Musical Fulfillment*. Ithaca, N.Y.: Cornell University Press, 1998.

Campbell, Margaret. *The Great Cellists*. North Pomfret, Vt.: Trafalgar Square Publishing, 1989.

Churchill, Bonnie. "Music: 'Inspired' Idea." *Boston Herald*. 29 March 1998.

Cowling, Elizabeth. *The Cello*. New York: Charles Scribner's Sons, 1975.

Davidson, Justin. "Have Cello, Will Travel." *Newsday*. 10 Nov. 1997.

Dyer, Richard. "Crossing Over Yo-Yo Makes Collaborative Music Films Out of Bach's Solo Cello Suites." *The Boston Globe*. 29 March 1998.

Eisler, Edith. "Continuity in Diversity." *Strings*. 1 May 2001.

Grotenhuis, Elizabeth Ten, ed. *Along the Silk Road*. Washington, D.C.: Smithsonian Institution, 2003.

Gurewitsch, Matthew. "Master Ma." *Town & Country*. February 1998.

Hirshey, Gerri. "We Are the World." *Parade*. 30 Jan. 2005.

Kenneson, Claude. *Musical Prodigies: Perilous Journeys, Remarkable Lives*. Portland, Ore.: Amadeus Press, 1998.

Levin, Theodore. *The Hundred Thousand Fools of God: Musical Travels in Central Asia*. Bloomington: Indiana University Press, 1996.

Lynn, Stacy, ed. *21st Century Cellists*. San Anselmo, Calif.: String Letter Publishing, 2001.

Ma, Marina, as told to John A. Rallo. *My Son, Yo-Yo*. Hong Kong: The Chinese University Press, 1995.

Osmond, Susan. "Yo-Yo Ma's Silk Road Project." *World and I*. April 2002.

Pincus, Andrew L. *Musicians with a Mission*. Boston: Northeastern University Press, 2002.

Stern, Isaac. *My First 79 Years*. New York: Alfred A. Knopf, 1999.

Stowell, Robin, ed. *The Cambridge Companion to the Cello*. New York: Cambridge University Press, 1999.

Whitefield, Susan. *Life Along the Silk Road*. Berkeley: University of California Press, 1999.

Ma, Yo-Yo. "A Journey of Discovery." *Program Book*. 2002 Smithsonian Folklife Festival. 24 Oct. 2006. www.silkroadproject.org/smithsonian/

"Yo-Yo Ma's Way with the Strings." *Time*. 19 Jan. 1981.

Africa, 52, 66–68
American Pageant of the Arts, An (television program), 11, 13
Appalachian fiddle music, 70
Appalachian Journey (album), 70
Appalachia Waltz (album), 70
Argentina, 71–73
Arthur (television program), 80
Aspen Music Festival, 55
Avery Fisher Prize, 58–59
Ax, Emanuel, 50, 61, 62

Bach, Anna Magdalena, 29
Bach, Johann Sebastian, 24, 25, 29, 32, 73–75
Bando, Tamasaburo, 75
bandoneon (instrument), 72
Beethoven, Ludwig van, 42, 82
Bernstein, Leonard, 11, 32
Boston Symphony Orchestra, 78
Botswana, 68
Brazil, 92
Buenos Aires, Argentina, 71
Bushmen, 52, 66–68

Carman, Owen, 43
Carnegie Hall, 30, 35
Carnegie Recital Hall, 41
Casals, Pablo, 32, 49
cello, 10, 62, 68, 70
"children's cello party," 80
Children's Orchestra Society, 31
China, 17–18, 19, 29, 85, 86, 88
Columbia University, 47–48
Communists, 29
crossover music, 66, 70, 73, 92
Crouching Tiger, Hidden Dragon (film), 83
cultural exchanges, 85, 86–88, 90–91, 92–94

Dan David Prize, 93
Davidoff Stradivarius, 62
Dean, Christopher, 75
Denmark, 94

De Vore, Irven, 52
Distant Echoes (documentary film), 67

Ecole Française, 33–35
electronic music, 65

fiddle music, 70

Goffriller, Matteo, 62
Grammy Awards, 63, 70, 73, 92

Harvard University, 48–49, 50–53, 56–58, 92
Hong Kong, 17, 18, 19
Hornor, Jill, 50–51, 56–58
horsehead fiddle (Mongolian instrument), 88
Hush (album), 66
hypercello, 65

Immortal Beloved (film), 81–82
improvisation, 66
Institute of Musical Art, 38
Israel, 93

John F. Kennedy Center for the Performing Arts, 13–14, 61
Juilliard School of Music, 37, 38, 47, 48

Kalahari Desert, Africa, 52, 66–68
Kaye, Danny, 11
Kennedy, Jacqueline, 10
Kennedy, John F., 10, 13
Kennedy Center, 13–14, 61

Levin, Theodore, 87
Liberty!: The American Revolution (television program), 82
Lincoln Center for the Performing Arts, 38, 59
Lo, Ya-Wen (mother), 17–20. *See also* Ma, Marina (mother).

Ma, Emily (daughter), 62

Ma, Hiao-Jone (uncle), 20, 28–29
Ma, Hiao-Tsiun (father), 17–21, 22–24,
    27–31, 32, 33–34, 35, 48, 56, 74,
    77
Ma, Marina (mother), 20, 22, 27, 31,
    35, 38–39, 48, 56. *See also* Lo,
    Ya-Wen (mother).
Ma, Nicholas (son), 62
Ma, Ya-Wen (mother), 20. *See also* Ma,
    Marina (mother).
Ma, Yeou-Cheng (sister), 9, 11–12, 13,
    20, 21, 22, 29, 31, 33, 35, 41
Ma, Yo-Yo
    on advice from Casals, 32
    as artist-in-residence, 57–58
    awards and honors, 58–59, 63, 70,
        73, 90, 92, 93–94
    birth of, 17
    on Casals, 32, 49
    on cultural exchanges, 85, 86
    discipline and, 38–39, 40, 43
    education of, 32–35, 38, 40, 42,
        47–48, 50–53
    effect of frequent performances
        on, 55
    expansion of musical repertoire
        of, 60, 61, 65–66, 69–73,
        90–92
    on exploring different musical
        cultures, 15
    favorite music of, 63
    on having children, 62
    on having surgery, 59
    health of, 59
    on his cello, 62
    on his mission, 94–95
    importance of, 14–15, 94
    on interpretation of music by
        artists, 74–75
    on Jill, 50
    marriage of, 56–58
    on master classes, 78–79
    meaning of name, 17
    on multiculturalism in upbringing,
        38, 52
    musical ability of, 21–22, 24
    at music camp, 43–45
    music during early childhood of,
        20–25
    music teachers of, 24, 32, 37–38,
        41–42, 47–48, 70
    on need to be alone, 40
    performances as adult by, 55–56,
        59–61, 89–90
    performances as child by, 9–13,
        14, 25, 29, 31, 32, 35
    performances as teenager by,
        41, 53
    performances for soundtracks,
        81–83
    on power of music, 77
    as recording artist, 62, 66, 70, 73,
        81–83, 90, 92
    on role of musician, 68
    as teacher, 57, 77–81, 92
    as teenager, 41–45, 47–53
    on teenage years of musicians, 78
    on television, 80–81
    travel and, 55, 59–61, 62, 89–90
    as United Nations peace
        ambassador, 94
    on violin, 23
Machover, Tod, 65
"Marco Polo of Music," 86
Marlboro Music Festival, 49–50
Marsalis, Wynton, 81, 82
master classes, 57, 78–80, 92
McFerrin, Bobby, 66
Meadowmount School of Music, 43–45
Mediterranean Sea, 85
Meyer, Edgar, 70
Mister Rogers' Neighborhood (televi-
    sion program), 80
Montagnana, Domenico, 62
morin khuur (Mongolian instrument),
    88, 91
multiculturalism, 38, 52
multiculturalism in music, 15, 85,
    86–88, 90, 92–94
museum partnerships, 92

Namibia, 67, 68
National Medal of the Arts, 90
National Symphony Orchestra, 11
New York City, 29–35, 37–38, 40–41
New York Times, The (newspaper), 13, 35, 41, 70
nomads, 68

Obrigado Brazil (album), 92
O'Connor, Mark, 70, 82

Paris, France, 17–20
piano, 22–23, 25
Piazzolla, Astor, 72–73
Polo, Marco, 86
Pré, Jacqueline du, 62
Professional Children's School, 40–41

Rhode Island School of Design, 92
Rice, Condoleeza, 90
Rochester, New York, 29
Rose, Leonard, 37–38, 41–42, 47–48, 77
Rose, Wendy, 45

Schleswig-Holstein Music Festival, 89
Scholz, Janos, 32, 37
Schweitzer, Albert, 75
scoliosis, 59
Sesame Street (television program), 80
Seven Years in Tibet (film), 82–83
Sheng, Bright, 88
Silk Road, 85–86, 88, 94
Silk Road Chicago, 94
Silk Road Ensemble, 88–89, 90, 92
Silk Road Journeys: When Strangers Meet (album), 90
Silk Road Project, 85, 86–88, 89, 91–93
Six Suites for Unaccompanied Cello

(Bach), 24, 25, 29
Sonning Music Prize, 94
Soul of the Tango—The Music of Astor Piazzolla (album), 73
soundtracks, 81–83
South Africa, 68
South America, 70–73, 92
Spoleto Festival USA, 55
Stern, Isaac, 28, 35, 37, 38, 48, 52, 77, 90

Tackling the Monster (video), 81
Tan Dun, 83
Tanglewood Music Center, 88
Tanglewood Music Festival, 55–56, 77–79
Tanglewood's Youth Orchestra, 77–79
tango, 71–73
Tonight Show, The (television program), 32
Torvill, Jayne, 75
Towson State University, 80
Trent School, 31
Tucker, Richard, 11

United Nations, 94

venturo (instrument of Bushmen), 68
violin, 22–23

Washington, D.C., 9–14
Washington Post, The (newspaper), 12
Williams, John, 82
World Cello Congress, 80

Yo-Yo Ma: Inspired by Bach (film series), 75

Myra Weatherly writes for children and young adults from her home in South Carolina. She found Yo-Yo Ma's story particularly exciting since her background includes teaching and publishing in the field of gifted education, as well as a graduate degree in Gifted Education.

Image Credits